W0010969

Made in the USA
Charleston, SC
19 January 2015

INTRODUCTION

My wife Rita is the best mom I have ever known. She is also the most consistent Christian I know, which bodes well with her mothering skills. What makes Rita unique in her relationship with our four daughters is her ability to balance between friendship and parenting. When the girls were growing up she connected daily with each girl in caring communication and affection, but she also gave them clear guidelines for behavior. Even to this day as adult children she talks with them often and offers advice when asked.

My mom Anita is a great mother as well. During my teenager years and the adolescent years of my two younger brothers, she raised us as a single parent. She work diligently in her domestic duties to care for three hungry—energized young men—and she worked outside the home cleaning houses and serving as a restaurant hostess in the evenings. Mother modeled for us optimism and hope during adversity and financial trials.

My mother-in-law Jean rounds out my three favorite mothers. Her unselfish service to her family motivates me to do the same for my family. She is always behind the scenes cooking, cleaning and making sure you feel cared for and loved. I have always felt like a son, as she remembers my birthday, anniversaries and meaningful milestones. My mother-in-law is an example of humility in the home and to everyone she meets.

Being a mother and wife is probably the hardest and most fulfilling role in the world. God's love and compassion flows through them like blood runs through the human body. Where would we be without moms? They are always there with a kind and encouraging word—ever thinking the best and wishing you well. Moms mother sons and daughters who rule nations, serve the poor, run companies, preach, teach and who grow up to be mothers and fathers. So, celebrate often the Lord's calling to be a mother for His glory!

"I prayed for this child, and the LORD has granted me what I asked of him. So now I give him to the LORD. For his whole life he will be given over to the LORD." And he worshiped the LORD there" (1 Samuel 1:27-28).

These 30 devotional readings for mothers are meant to encourage, instruct and comfort. A woman can have down mothering techniques, but they must be based on a deep trust in Jesus Christ. He is your identity and security. So, the over arching goal of Wisdom for Mothers is to engage you into a deep and loving relationship with your Heavenly Father. A mother who is loved well—loves well!

"We always thank God, the Father of our Lord Jesus Christ, when we pray for you, because we have heard of your faith in Christ Jesus and of the love you have for all God's people— the faith and love that spring from the hope stored up for you in heaven and about which you have already heard in the true message of the gospel that has come to you. In the same way, the gospel is bearing fruit and growing throughout the whole world—just as it has been doing among you since the day you heard it and truly understood God's grace" (Colossians 1:3-6).

TABLE OF CONTENTS

1

Mothers Show Up

Near the cross of Jesus stood his mother, his mother's sister, Mary the wife
of Clopas, and Mary Magdalene. When Jesus saw his mother there,
and the disciple whom he loved standing nearby, he said to his mother,
"Dear woman, here is your son," and to the disciple, "Here is your mother."
From that time on, this disciple took her into his home.
John 19:25-27

Mothers show up. They show up at the birth of their child. They show up when the baby wakes up, cries, is hungry or needs changing. Moms show up at the bus stop, in the car pool line, at teacher conferences, as homeroom moms and at ball games. They show up to wash their child's clothes, clean their rooms, help with homework and feed their bellies.

The Lord put relentless and forgiving love in the heart of mothers. Moms cannot, not care for their child, because this is how Christ made them. Why does a godly mom show up in quiet supplication for the soul of their son or daughter? Why does a woman of God go to church faithfully with their child in tow, so they can hear the truth about Jesus' love?

These women of faith keep showing up on behalf of their Savior, because like the mother of Jesus, they love Jesus. The love of Christian moms flows out of the love for their Lord. Their Heavenly Father first loves them, so they in turn can deeply love their loved ones with the Lord's everlasting love. Indeed, you show up to be loved by Jesus, so you can show up to love for Jesus. Mothers who love their children best are first loved by Christ.

"I have been reminded of your sincere faith, which first lived in your grandmother Lois and in your mother Eunice and, I am persuaded, now lives in you also" (2 Timothy 1:5).

Lastly, loving moms show up during the darkest days of sorrow. They keep coming back to the bedside of their little one languishing with illness. The stamina of a mom over her sick child sometimes seems supernatural—and it is—because the Holy Spirit is their supply. He is there to give you the support you need to be the mom Christ has called you to be. Stay true to showing up with your Savior each day. He will equip and empower you to be the mom for your children. Show up for Jesus and He will show up for you to be the mom for your children. Show up for Jesus and He will show up for you.

"I prayed for this child, and the LORD has granted me what I asked of him. So now I give him to the LORD. For his whole life he will be given over to the LORD." And he worshiped the LORD there" (1 Samuel 1:27-28).

Do I allow the Lord to love me, so I can better love my child?

Related Readings: 1 Samuel 2:1-11; 2 Kings 4:29-30; Mark 3:31; 1 Thessalonians 2:7

2

Leave and Cleave

"Haven't you read," he replied, "that at the beginning the Creator 'made them male and female,' and said, 'For this reason a man will leave his father and mother and be united to his wife, and the two will become one flesh'? So they are no longer two, but one. Therefore what God has joined together, let man not separate."
Matthew 19:4-6

It's hard for parents to give away their child in marriage. It's easy for parents to give away their child in marriage. These are mixed emotions that most fathers and mothers feel on the wedding day of their baby. I am happy the Lord brought the bride and groom together in holy matrimony, but I am sad to see them go. There is a hole in my heart.

But, from the beginning our Creator made them male and female for the purpose of becoming one flesh. God's desire for oneness with married couples can only happen by leaving father and mother and cleaving to Christ and one another. It is sad to see them go, but there is gladness—knowing they will grow in grace and in love for one another.

"But grow in the grace and knowledge of our Lord and Savior Jesus Christ. To . im be glory both now and forever! Amen" (2 Peter 3:18).

In fact, our child is limited in their understanding of the Lord, if they remain under our roof. For their faith to become more real and robust they must become their own man or woman. Faith is meant to flourish from the foundation of a Christ-centered marriage. They become one flesh in Christ, so they can learn to passionately follow the Lord and serve others. Parents have the privilege of letting their child leave well and cleave well.

Therefore, trust God with the transition of your child into young adulthood. Do not hamper their growth by hovering, but hold them with an open hand, and watch the grace of God grow them into trophies of His truth. Let them go and let them grow. The hole in your heart means you love them so much, so love large and let the Lord fill your hole of sadness with His cup of gladness. Cleave to Christ, as they leave and cleave to one other!

"But cleave unto the LORD your God, as ye have done unto this day" (Joshua 23:8 KJV).

Do I hold my child with an open hand? Am I cleaving to my spouse and Christ alone?

Related Readings: Deuteronomy 11:22; Judges 1:13; Acts 11:23; Romans 12:9-10

3

A Fruitful Family

Blessed are all who fear the Lord, who walk in . is ways. You will eat the fruit
of your labor; blessings and prosperity will be yours. Your wife will be like a
fruitful vine within your house; your sons will be like olive shoots around your
table. Thus is the man blessed who fears the Lord.
Psalm 128:1-4

The fruit from a family who fears the Lord is tasty and delicious. However, this type of fruit does not happen immediately, but is cultivated over time. A fruitful wife sets the tone for the home. By God's grace she weeds out criticism and replaces it with creativity. The home is her "pride and joy". It is a reflection of her, as it is her nest.

A home to the wife is like an office to the husband. Things need to be just right or she feels violated. Indeed, be grateful for a conscientious wife who wants to express herself through the home. The fruit of a clean, decorated and ordered home is calming. It provides an environment of stability and frees family members to focus on each other and people. A husband is free to do what he does best at work with a supportive wife at home.

A mother's influence spreads like a lovely vine throughout the house. No area is left untouched. The children are nurtured and encouraged by her sensitivity. When instilled from birth, the fruit from children become obedience to God and love for the Lord. Their heart for God grows when parents read Bible stories to them, as they wait in the womb.

The warm embrace of their little arms around your neck is the fruit of trust. The look of their kind and trusting eyes is the fruit of consistent love from mom and dad. Their bent toward love for God and people is fruit from their parent's example of following Jesus.

Furthermore, family fruit flourishes when the man of the house models faithfulness. A husband's intentional effort to follow the Lord ignites faith at home. A fruitful wife has no problem submitting to a husband who submits to God. A God fearing man is quick to confess sin to his Heavenly father and to his family. It is not uncommon for him to say, "I am sorry" or "I was wrong". Authentic confession encourages confession in others.

Confessed up hearts are family fruit. It is probable the family will pray, read their Bible and go to church, if the leader of the home does the same. Family fruit has a direct correlation to the faithfulness of the family head. Family fruit flourishes when the man fears God. Regardless of the circumstances he is committed to doing what God expects.

Therefore, your home becomes a hot house of character. The fruit threatens to bust through the glass panels for all to see. People are encouraged when they visit your hospitable home. Sinners need a safe environment, as acceptance comes from the fruit of Christ's acceptance. Heaven's dew and rainfall keep the fruit coming to a home submitted to Christ. Jesus says, "This is to my Father's glory, that you bear much fruit, showing yourselves to be my disciples" (John 15:8). Fruit is proof of faithful families.

Does my character cultivate fruit that glorifies God in my family?

Related Readings: Genesis 7:1; Proverbs 31:15; Mark 5:19; Acts 10:2

4

Marvelously Made

Ears that hear and eyes that see—the Lord has made them both.
Proverbs 20:12

Our bodies are marvelously made, which means we have a marvelous Maker. How could there be such precision and complexity, without a supreme Creator in Christ? The human body is grand evidence for Almighty God. We are created by God, and we are created for God. The Almighty is the architect of our flesh, so our actions reflect Him. "Does He who implanted the ear not hear? Does He who formed the eye not see?" (Psalm 94:9).

Our feet are designed to walk by faith down familiar and unfamiliar paths of righteousness. Our eyes keep an eye on eternity, always aware of the Almighty's accountability. Our ears listen to the voice of the Holy Spirit and obey His commands. Our hands are quick to serve others in the name of Jesus Christ.

Your body is a billboard for belief in the Lord, so take care to present Christ with correct and consistent conduct. "I praise you because I am fearfully and wonderfully made; your works are wonderful, I know that full well" (Psalm 139:14). Every muscle, nerve and fiber of our being is bold to proclaim praise to its Creator for His creation.

It is in wonder and awe that a child of God worships in thanks for His grand plan, the body. You witness the gestation of life in the womb of a loved one, and your instincts feel instructed by God. He originates life and determines death. All parts of your frame your Heavenly Father has fashioned and formed.

Therefore, exclaim with adoration and thanksgiving to God for the beauty of His beings. Your body is a testament to the truth of His existence. Use it to point others to Jesus. Abuse it, and you poorly manage your Makers physical phenomena. Your body is a bold exclamation of eternal consequences.

"But blessed are your eyes because they see, and your ears because they hear" (Matthew 13:6).

How can I use my body, so others better understand Christ? Does my body take me to places and people pleasing to Him?

Related Readings: Psalm 119:18; Proverbs 18:15; Acts 26:18; Ephesians 1:17-18

5

Attentive To Children

Samuel continued as judge over Israel all the days of his life. From year to year he went on a circuit from Bethel to Gilgal to Mizpah, judging Israel in all those places... But his sons did not walk in his ways. They turned aside after dishonest gain and accepted bribes and perverted justice.
1 Samuel 7:15-16, 8:3

Children need attention. They spell love, T-I-M-E. We can be so busy, even busy doing good things; that we miss out on God's best, which is spending time with our children. They need time to laugh and time to cry, time to run and jump; and time to be still and nap. Children need time to pray, go to the library, and make snow angels, ski, and play dolls, dress up, make believe, play in the dirt, climb trees and play hid and seek.

Parents have the tremendous privilege to invest time in their child, to have dates, hunt and shop together. You can take trips, run on the beach; chase sand crabs, swim and watch the sun go down. You can eat a peanut butter sandwich and pretzels at their school; attend their sporting events and proudly watch their school play or awards ceremony.

If we miss our children experiencing life, we neglect them. If we neglect our children, there is a high probability they will reject us and/or our faith. Indeed, their perception of dad and mom is their perception of God. If we are distant, uninvolved and disengaged, so they will see their Heavenly Father. Therefore invest time, money and love in your child.

Children require. and in some cases demand, a lot of attention. Your role is to be there for them, to be available. Your quality time with your child flows from your quantity time with them. You cannot stage or script quality time. It just happens, and you have to be around them to enjoy its benefit. When children are comfortable, they open up; sometimes unexpectedly they begin to share their heart. These spontaneous snippets of time become precious teachable moments. Remember quality time requires quantity time.

For example, after attending their sporting event, affirm and encourage them. They already know about their mistakes, they just need to know everything is ok, and they will do better next time. The most important part is showing up. You are the first person they look for in the crowd. When you are there, it shows you care. You cannot make up for these childhood days, but there will be other deals, work projects, ministry roles and business opportunities. Be careful to not let work or ministry compete with your family.

When at all possible integrate two competing responsibilities. It may mean a family mission trip or serving together in the church nursery. If work requires travel take a child with you and make it a special trip with just the two of you. Let your child watch you "do life", let them see you trusting God with a difficult situation, or watch you give Him credit for a great success. Then as they mature into adults, your child feels accepted rather than neglected, they respect mom and dad, and they embrace faith in Jesus.

How does my child like to spend time with me? Does my calendar and checkbook reflect dedicated time with my child?

Related Readings: Deuteronomy 6:6-7; Judges 14:3-4; Luke 2:41-52; Hebrews 11:23

6

Youth Discipleship

Remember your Creator in the days of your youth, before the days of trouble come and the years approach when you will say, "I find no pleasure in them"...
Ecclesiastes 12:1

The heart of a child, student and young adult is impressionable. Like moist clay in the hands of an artist, it is pliable and moldable. This is the time to train and teach a youthful heart in the ways of Christ. It is on the solid foundation of the Lord's precepts and principles that life and death make sense. A young memory of God remembers God.

"I have been reminded of your sincere faith, which first lived in your grandmother Lois and in your mother Eunice and, I am persuaded, now lives in you also" (2 Timothy 1:5).

His hope is alive and everlasting for the young at heart. We need young people who are world changers, who believe they can make a difference. Those of us who have been around a while need to encourage their zeal for living and their optimism for engaging opportunities and people. Commission them to travel the globe, while being under girded by the Word of God. The Lord looks to the young of heart to ignite a revival of prayer.

Your opportunities as a young person are staggering. Your greatest leverage will come as you dive deep in your relationship with God and people. Channel your youthful energy and passion toward an intimate love relationship with your Heavenly Father. Your earthly father may be distant or non-existent, but not God. He is there for you 24/7. He longs to walk with you through these days of multiple transitions, challenges and growth.

Do not miss God. Your relationship with Him sets the pace for other relationships. If you want relational security, learn how from the lover of your soul—Jesus. If you want peace in your relationships, then become a student of the Prince of Peace. If you desire to better understand people, then hang out with their Creator who fully understands them. Youth is your asset not your liability. Do not be ashamed, but be confident in Christ.

"Don't let anyone look down on you because you are young, but set an example for the believers in speech, in life, in love, in faith and in purity" (1 Timothy 4:12).

As an adult you have tremendous influence on youth. It may be formal education, like paying tuition to a school that aligns with your values and beliefs. Maybe you can volunteer at church educating the children and youth. Graduate beyond babysitting, to instilling the truth of God at all levels of childhood and teenage development.

Teach the young to obey God, to love God, and to give away God to others. Memorize Scripture together in song and by writing out His word. Help them learn how to study and understand the Bible. Hang out with them in high adventure and outdoor camp settings. Provide these teachable environments as a laboratory for their faith in Jesus Christ.

Disciple young people early on so they can be examples for Christ. Their spiritual growth will not happen by accident. Help them to understand "why" they believe "what" they believe. Move them way beyond sterile religion to a robust relationship with Jesus. If the young remember their Creator and follow His ways. everyone is successful. Therefore, remember your Creator and lead the youth to do the same. God memories matter most.

"They remembered that God was their Rock, that God Most High was their Redeemer" (Psalm 78:35).

Do I often remember my Creator? What young person can I invest in the ways of God?

Related Readings: Proverbs 22:6; Isaiah 46:9; Ephesians 2:11-13; Titus 2:4

Daily Wisdom in Your Inbox... A Free Subscription: **www.wisdomhunters.com**

7

Start Young

For you have been my hope, O Sovereign Lord, my confidence since my youth... Since my youth, O God, you have taught me, and to this day I declare your marvelous deeds.
Psalm 71:5, 17

Start young learning the ways of the Lord. This is your wisest and best investment. Youthful learning is leverage for the Lord. Start young so you do not have to wade through the muck and the mire of disobedient living. There is no need to stray and go your own way for you may end up back at the point where you originally drifted from God. Stay the course of Christ while you are young, and this will catapult you into an obedient adult. Youthful dependence on God results in an adult who depends on God.

Even as those older in the faith falter in fear, your heavenly Father frees youthful hearts to attempt big things for Him. Courage and conviction fertilize well a young and hungry heart for God. The Holy Spirit is calling faithful young people to further His Kingdom. Listen to the heart of your heavenly Father and do what He says. Yahweh is calling His youth to something much bigger than themselves.

"Let no man despise thy youth; but be thou an example of the believers, in word, in conversation, in charity, in spirit, in faith, in purity" (1 Timothy 4:12, KJV).

Help the youthful start early in their engagement with God. Teach them, train them, model for them, and then send them out to serve on the Lord's behalf. Youth do not need to be overly protected, but set free to think big for God. The larger the vision the larger their God, therefore present to them a God-sized challenge. Expect great things from young people who have a heart to follow hard after God.

Do not underestimate their ability to be a catalyst for Christ. Release them to exceed your accomplishments in half the time. Pray for God to scatter young people across the connected planet. Now is the time to send them out in the power of the Holy Spirit. Use today's resources to prepare for tomorrow's results. Youth need not be coddled with the status quo, rather challenged to break out of their boxes of unbelief to change the world.

"Remember your Creator in the days of your youth, before the days of trouble come and the years approach when you will say, "I find no pleasure in them" (Ecclesiastes 12:1).

What young person has God brought into my life to invest in with time, wisdom and encouragement?

Related Readings: Numbers 11:28; Job 13:26; Psalm 25:7; 2 Timothy 2:22

8

Respect Him

The wife must respect her husband.
Ephesians 5:33b

Respect for a husband is like love is for a wife. It is a catalyst for his confidence and encouragement that he can fulfill his role as provider and leader. Most men question their ability to be everything they need to be for their family. But insecurities become insignificant in a home where a husband feels respect. A wife's support energizes her man like jet fuel to a booster rocket.

Husbands need the respect and support of their wives. It of course works both ways, as the wife needs to feel the support of her husband. But, respect is huge for a man. A God-fearing husband knows the Lord has placed him in a position of leadership. It is overwhelming sometimes because of feeling squeezed from the pressures of life. The last thing a husband needs to feel is distance or distrust from his wife. Her spousal support may be the only thing that is preventing him from giving up.

"He must manage his own family well and see that his children obey him, and he must do so in a manner worthy of full respect" (1 Timothy 3:4).

Wives: Do not underestimate how your support sustains your husband. Your affirmation is valuable and powerful for the ongoing success of your husband. Men are not as self-sufficient as they might seem. On the outside we may seem invincible, but on the inside we are needy and desperate for recognition and validation. A man needs to know his wife trusts his decision-making and his ability to provide for his family.

Your confidence in him propels his confidence in himself to higher levels. Your belief in your husband builds him up to believe in himself. It is difficult for a man to rise any higher than the opinion of his helpmate. Men long to be built up by their brides. Brag on him in public and affirm him in private. Look to your husband as the leader God has placed in your life.

Pray for him to lead lovingly and wisely. Be patient and don't usurp his authority when things are not getting done. Trust him to God, for He can handle him much better than your creative consequences. Give him over to God and trust in the accountability of the Almighty. Embrace your husband in the light of eternity. God wants him to grow up and give spiritual leadership. Let him lead—even when it means he fails. Your respect can grow the heart of your husband to love well.

"Give to everyone what you owe them: If you owe taxes, pay taxes; if revenue, then revenue; if respect, then respect; if honor, then honor" (Romans 13:7).

How can I respect my husband in a way that encourages him and also honors the Lord?

Related Readings: Deuteronomy 1:15; Proverbs 31:23; Luke 11:43; 1 Timothy 3:2-4

9

Spiritual Resources

A shoot will come up from the stump of Jesse: from his roots a Branch will bear fruit. The
Spirit of the Lord will rest on him—the Spirit of wisdom and understanding,
the Spirit of counsel and of power, the Spirit of knowledge and of
the fear of the Lord—and he will delight in the fear of the Lord.
Isaiah 11:1-3a

God provides spiritual resources for His children—all we need is in Christ. The same Spirit of the Lord that indwelled and empowered Jesus is the One who does the same for His followers. The Son of God indwells us by faith—the spirit of God rests on us and in us. The Holy Spirit provides all the spiritual resources needed to carry out His will.

You need wisdom; He provides good judgment. You need understanding; He provides discernment. You need counsel; He provides advice. You need power; He provides strength. You need knowledge; He provides information. You need the fear of God; He provides holy awe. However, resources without reception are without results.

I can offer to take my daughter shopping, but if she chooses to attend a movie with her friend instead, she will miss her daddy buying her some cute clothes. It is in a moment in time that God offers you His resources. Don't be so wrapped up in your plan that you miss His provision. Everyday the resources you need are a prayer away.

Wisdom, understanding and His godly counsel are all there for the asking. The same Spirit of God that indwelled and empowered Jesus does the same for you. The Holy Spirit is at your side to convict, comfort and guide. "But the Counselor, the Holy Spirit, whom the Father will send in my name, will teach you all things and will remind you of everything I have said to you" (John 14:26). Thus, solicit the Spirit to lead you.

Jesus is our friend and Savior. God is our Father and Lord. The Spirit is our guide and counselor. The Holy Spirit will guide you in truth and righteousness. You cannot see the Spirit of God, but you can experience His affects. The Spirit is what puts a check in your spirit to protect you from an unwise choice. The Spirit is what empowers your spirit to faith and courage. Allow the Holy Spirit to congeal with your spirit. Do not relegate Him to some obscure corner of your life, just because you do not totally understand Him.

Furthermore, the fruit of the Spirit will flow from your life as He is unleashed by faith. Love, joy, peace, patience, kindness, goodness, faithfulness, gentleness and self-control are the fruit bearing consequences of the Holy Spirit's control. What He does is ripe, wonderful and appealing to the eyes and tasteful to the tongue. Your relationship with your Heavenly Father is not complete without your empowerment of the Holy Spirit.

This is where unremarkable religion can become a rejuvenated relationship. If your relationship with God is in a rut then let the Holy Spirit fall fresh on your life. Start by allowing the fruit of the Spirit to mold your character. Be accountable to fruit inspectors in your life. Let these honest more mature friends help you purge back fruitless attitudes and actions. Prune the bad to make room for the good. Unpack and use the Spirit's gifts.

God has gifted you uniquely. Allow His gifts to develop and come to full fruition. This is good stewardship for an undeveloped gift may go away. If you are gifted to teach, teach. If you are gifted to write, write. If you are gifted to lead, lead. If you are gifted to mentor, mentor. If you are gifted to give, give. The Spirit of God rests on you and dwells in you. By faith, allow the Spirit to develop your character and competence into bushels of fruit.

"You did not choose me, but I chose you and appointed you to go and bear fruit—fruit that will last. Then the Father will give you whatever you ask in my name. This is my command: Love each other" (John 15:16-17).

Do I daily invite the fullness of the Spirit to fill me with faith, hope and love?

Related Readings: Genesis 41:38; Exodus 35:31; Galatians 5:16-26; 1 John 4:2-3

Daily Wisdom in Your Inbox... A Free Subscription: **www.wisdomhunters.com**

10

Total Trust

Surely God is my salvation; I will trust and not be afraid. The Lord, the Lord,
is my strength and my song;. e has become my salvation. With joy you will
draw water from the wells of salvation.
Isaiah 12:2-3

Total trust in God means total confidence in Christ's character, which is available to every faithful follower of Jesus. Total trust means we give up total control. It is a wise trade that reaps radical results. Christ's control replaces fear with peace. We do not have to figure it all out—instead we trust God. We aren't capable to know all, but we do have capacity to totally trust Him. Do I utterly trust Him with everything? "Trust in the LORD with all your heart and lean not on your own understanding" (Proverbs 3:5).

If Christ is who He claimed to be—He can be trusted. Jesus said, "Anyone who has seen me has seen the Father" (John 14:9b). If we can trust Him with the eternal salvation of our soul, we can trust Him with the temporal control of our life. If we can trust Him with the big things like faith in Jesus, we can trust Him with the small things like fear of man.

If He leads you to a new career He will give you the wisdom, finances and relationships to be successful. If He leads you to be a missionary He will build bridges across the cultural barriers that allow you to serve and love the people. If He leads you to have children, He will provide the needed resources to be successful parents.

Wherever God leads—He provides. What God initiates—He completes. His part is provision and our part is trust. Don't fall into the trap of trusting Him with some things and not trusting Him with others. Distrust in God is distasteful. It is an insult to His integrity. How can God not be big enough to handle any situation? Health issues, war, teenagers, money, conflict, prosperity, relationships and uncertainty can all be placed into God's hands—not to be taken back. Total trust means we leave it in the Lord's care.

God can be trusted because He is trustworthy. The waters of His salvation bubble up from an infinitely deep well. So your thirsty soul can always drink and be satisfied. Without the support of a sympathetic Jesus you will be immobilized—even crushed—under the weight of worry, but Jesus is there to outsource your anxiety. Be with Him.

"Come to me, all you who are weary and burdened, and I will give you rest. Take my yoke upon you and learn from me, for I am gentle and humble in heart, and you will find rest for your souls. For my yoke is easy and my burden is light" (Matthew 11:28-30).

Trust in Christ means to prayerfully walk with Him in your choices. Slow down, look up, trust Him and watch Him create extraordinary results. Partial trust leads to frustration and worry, but total trust leads to contentment and calm. Joy occupies fully trusting the Lord. Your soul sings in thanksgiving and an inner peace from Jesus strengthens your faith.

Jesus said, "Peace I leave with you; my peace I give you. I do not give to you as the world gives. Do not let your hearts be troubled and do not be afraid" (John 14:27).

Do I trust Christ only when it is convenient, or do I totally trust Him at all times?

Related Readings: Exodus 14:31; 2 Samuel 7:28; Acts 14:23; Revelation 22:6

11

Forced Rest

He makes me lie down in green pastures,
he leads me beside quiet waters.
Psalm 23:2

Sometimes the Lord makes His children create margin in their lives. He understands that a life without real rest can become graceless and grumpy. It may be physical illness, emotional overload, spiritual fatigue or ruptured relationships that begin to scream for attention. The flesh thinks it can continue with little or no rest, but the spirit knows better.

We may work through our fatigue and fake it for a while, but eventually we hit an unscalable wall, without anything to give anymore. Jesus knows we are extra vulnerable during these tired times and He makes a way of retreat and rest. His gentle and loving care calls us to come apart with Him. It's much better to heed His invitation for intimacy than to move down the road without Him. Resting in the Lord invigorates and inspires.

Does rest have to be mandated by our Master or can it be done willfully? A wise man or woman understands the need for rhythms of rest in their schedule. This is why a good night's sleep and occasional naps are necessary. Weekends, especially Sundays are made for rest, reflection and rejuvenation. If we are intoxicated by activity, we run the risk of living in a restless hangover. Real rest allows us to recover and unwind in His presence.

Like green pastures are pleasant and fulfilling for any animal dependent on the earth, so God's heavenly resources feed our soul, fill our mind and hydrate our heart. Are you tired and overwhelmed? Do you feel alone and deplete of any energy to engage with others? If so, take the time to get away with God. Say no to the unnecessary and yes to the necessary. The most productive life accomplishes more by doing less. It rests in Him.

Most importantly, allow the Lord to lead you by faith into a quiet place. Sit by the soothing silence of still waters and drink in the majesty of God's creation. You know Jesus is leading you—when you intentionally engage in solitude for the purpose of hearing His voice. Lie on His green grass and look up, so your gaze is on God. Don't resist His required rest—instead cease and desist activity, embrace and celebrate His rest.

"When I consider Your heavens, the work of Your fingers, the moon and the stars, which You have set in place, what is man that you are mindful of him, the son of man that you care for him?" (Psalm 8:3-4). The grandeur of God's glory comes down to care for you.

Do I voluntarily engage with eternity in quiet places? Does my life rhythm require rest?

Related Readings: Exodus 31:13; 2 Samuel 22:33-34; Zechariah 10:1; Romans 9:11

12

Author of Change

Forget the former things; do not dwell on the past.
See I am doing a new thing! Now it springs up; do you not perceive
it? I am making a way in the desert and streams in the wasteland.
Isaiah 43:18-19

God is the original change agent. The past is past, as He is interested in new things. New relationships, new life, new endeavors, new learning, new languages, new cultures, new methods, new character, new ways of doing things is on the heart of God. He never changes, but what He does transforms. "I the LORD do not change" (Malachi 3:6a).

His Spirit is on the move, initiating all the time. His work is never totally complete. God is a master at taking nothing and making something. He can take new and raw talent and craft it into a Christ honoring home or career. The grim times of yesterday He replaces with the potential of today. Do not be afraid to start over with our God of second chances.

He can take your desert experience and build beautiful aqua ducts of grace. He wants to do a new work in your life. He wants you to change. Christ is your change agent. The old habits of anger and unforgiveness can and will be changed by the work of the Holy Spirit in you. A surrendered life is always under the influence of righteous transformation.

"And we, who with unveiled faces all reflect the Lord's glory, are being transformed into His likeness with ever-increasing glory, which comes from the Lord, who is the Spirit" (2 Corinthians 3:18).

God is the father of change, but He wants to use you as a change agent as well. You can become God's representative for change—a revolutionary for righteousness. There are new things that need to happen in your family, work and church. You have been a spectator long enough. It is time you engaged as a participant. You have properly prepared, now others look to you for leadership. Prayerfully make wise changes.

You will lead your family through this valley. Your response to adversity will be their response to adversity. If you are calm and trusting, then they will be calm and trusting. If you embrace change, then they will embrace change. Change can shake everyone out of their complacency and move them forward in Christ. Embrace and celebrate change.

You may be the change agent for your church. The church needs to change from irrelevant methods to ones that captivate the culture. And lastly your work needs an extreme makeover. It is through your humble influence that change is taking place. Submit to Christ's changes in your life, so you can be His change agent in the culture.

"But now, by dying to what once bound us, we have been released from the law so that we serve in the new way of the Spirit, and not in the old way of the written code" (Romans 7:6).

Am I allowing my unchanging Savior Jesus to change me? Am I a catalyst for change?

Related Readings: 1 Samuel 10:9, Psalm 55:19, 1 Corinthians 11:25, Hebrews 10:20

13

A Mother's Love

As apostles of Christ we could have been a burden to you,
but we were gentle among you, like a mother caring for her little children.
1 Thessalonians 2:7

A mother's love reflects the love of the Lord, deep in its capacity and generous in its application. She awakes in the middle of the night to nurse a hungry infant, or care for a sick child. Her intuition injects love at points of pain, and in situations that require extensive encouragement. A mother's love lingers long in conversation and understands with her sensitive heart. She loves, because Christ's love compels her to love like Him.

Moreover, a mother's love is loyal and longstanding. A child may be in trouble, but mom is always close by full of compassion and acceptance. Her love can be blind in its loyalty, but her offspring never doubt where they are welcome. Jesus was rejected by angry, jealous men and abandoned by His closest friends, but His mother was waiting with Him to the bitter end, "Near the cross of Jesus stood his mother... (John 19:25a).

A mother's love even has the capacity to be a mother to those who are not biologically her own. Amazingly she can informally 'adopt' people for a season and love on them emotionally, physically, spiritually and relationally. She opens her home, shares her food, gives her time, dispenses her wisdom, and encourages obedience to follow Christ. Paul experienced this, "Greet Rufus, chosen in the Lord, and his mother, who has been a mother to me, too" (Romans 16:13). Moms sometime mother greatness not their own.

Lastly, a mother's love is gentle like God is gentle toward His children. He calls us to love and to lead like Jesus. Love serves people and does not rule with rigor. "God's servant must not be argumentative, but a gentle listener and a teacher who keeps cool, working firmly but patiently with those who refuse to obey" (2 Timothy 2:24, TM)

Do I model gentle and patient love? Do others feel safe to share their sorrows with me?

Related Readings: Genesis 47:12; Ruth 4:16; John 21:15-17; James 3:17

14

Comfort and Joy

Shout for joy, O heavens; rejoice, O earth; burst into song, O mountains!
For the Lord comforts his people and will have compassion on his afflicted ones.
Isaiah 49:13

God is aware of our suffering and He wants His children to discover relief in Him. Our affliction may be self-inflicted or from outside sources. Regardless, His compassion is more than empathy, but active and far reaching. No matter how deep and severe our wounds, He cares. He comforts the afflicted and afflicts those who are too comfortable.

He understands your hurt. He understands your rejection. He understands your humiliation. He understands your fears. Jesus walked through the hurt of humanity on His way to the hallelujahs of heaven. He will never leave you or forsake you. It is for you and others that He lived and died. His mercies, love and grace are new every morning. "Because of the LORD's great love we are not consumed, for his compassions never fail. They are new every morning; great is your faithfulness" (Lamentations 3:22-23).

Christ is a catalyst for community, as He invites you to join Him and His church. The compassion of Christ and others is a healing balm; so seek out the comfort and compassion of God's people. The Body of Christ is there to administer healing and support. A wounded body part will eventually die if left unattended, but will recover and thrive with the support of other members. Christians are interdependent on one another.

Pride resists receiving help, but humility seeks help. Pride and humility cannot coexist. Pride says I can buck up and go at this alone. Humility says alone I will fail, but with others I will succeed. Our perception becomes skewed under the onslaught of affliction. We lose sight of the spiritual battle that is raging. Humility battles on its knees in prayer.

But your brothers and sisters in Christ help you fight the enemy, like loyal comrades in a crisis. So, let God's comfort and the comfort of others administer grace to your wounded heart. Trust Him to fight the good fight on your behalf. Let Jesus love on you. Let people encourage you and hold you accountable. One day you will be able to comfort others with the same comfort you have received. Indeed, your compassion will be much deeper, broader and Christ-like. Therefore, rejoice because of His great comfort and compassion!

"Praise be to the God and Father of our Lord Jesus Christ, the Father of compassion and the God of all comfort, who comforts us in all our troubles, so that we can comfort those in any trouble with the comfort we ourselves receive from God" (2 Corinthians 1:3-4).

Do I rejoice in the comfort of Christ? Am I extending His comfort to the uncomfortable?

Related Readings: Psalm 119:50-52; Isaiah 12:1; 2 Corinthians 7:7; Philippians 2:1-3

15

Work of Art

So I went down to the potter's house, and I saw him working at the wheel.
But the pot he was shaping from the clay was marred in his hands,
so the potter formed it into another pot, shaping it as seemed best to
him... Like the clay in the hand of the potter, so are you in my hand...
Jeremiah 18:3, 6b

We are God's work of art. If we are a follower of Jesus Christ then God owns us. He is the potter and we are the clay. Our life is destined to be a masterpiece in the hands of our Master Jesus. It requires a lifetime of molding and shaping, but our life after experiencing the grace of God is most attractive than before God's grace governed our life.

There are a least two prerequisites of a life masterpiece molded by God. One is a masterful artist and the other is moist clay. One without the other is doomed for failure. A gifted artist can be motivated and available, but without a subject he only works in his imagination. A person can long to be the object of an artist's inspiration, but there must be a relationship for them to benefit.

God is the artist and you are His subject. His part is to mold and create. Your part is to be available and teachable. This is how your Master works. He needs your life coupled with your undivided attention and your moldable heart and mind. Dry and brittle clay is useless in the hand of the potter. It cracks under pressure and gives in to discomfort.

However, clay that is moist and moldable is full of potential. In the beginning the sticky mire is hard on the eyes and uninviting, but over time it begins to take shape. The molding process is not easy. Sometimes you feel discombobulated and shapeless. You know God is in control, but your circumstances have you feeling upside down and spiraling out of control. This is God's wheel of wisdom. Uncertainty and dizziness is God's opportunity to grip the dampened clay of your heart and form dependence on Him.

Feel His fingers of compassion, hope and holiness. He not only comforts you, but also conforms you into the image of His son Jesus. He has the big picture in mind as He looks down on the potter's wheel. Your perspective is limited as you look up from the clay soaked wheel peering up into the faithful face of the potter. "For those God foreknew . e also predestined to be conformed to the image of His Son" (Romans 8:29a).

He is passionate about His work of art. Out of billions in the world you are His unique masterpiece. You are His one and only. He broke the mold on you and every one else. No one is quite like you. No one! Yes, He is still smoothing up rough edges and spinning out impediments to His will. Your life stays moldable through humility and teachability.

Sometimes it is the water of adversity that keeps the clay moist. Other times it is success that dampens the dirt. Whatever God is using to mold your character do not resist. Let Him process your life through His caressing and caring hands. It is better to be in the hands of God, spinning in uncertainty, than to be on our own, risk-less and rest-less. You are a beautiful masterpiece in process that one-day will be completed by your Creator.

"But who are you, a human being, to talk back to God? "Shall what is formed say to the one who formed it, 'Why did you make me like this?'" Does not the potter have the right to make out of the same lump of clay some pottery for special purposes and some for common use" (Romans 9:20-21)?

Do I willingly submit to my Master's molding me into the character of Christ?

Related Readings: Isaiah 29:15-16; 45:9; 64:8; Matthew 10:29-31; Philippians 3:20

16

Audience of One

I love the Father and do exactly what my Father has commanded me.
John 14:31b

I struggle playing to an audience other than Almighty God. I create an unnecessary tension by asking myself, "What will they think? How will they respond?" Yet the heart of Jesus asks, "What does my heavenly Father want? How can I obey Him with my whole heart?" It is an audience of one with my heavenly Father that requires my focus.

So I ask myself, "Whom do I love more?" Do I love my savior more, or do I love the praise of people more? If I truly love the commendation of Christ more than the approval of people then I will obey His commands, even when I am misunderstood and mistreated. A life that loves God longs to grow in a relationship that faithfully follows His ways.

But there is a caution to not become proud about our obedience. In a distorted way a disciplined life can play into impressing people instead of pleasing God. It is false humility to be proud of our humility and wish others could attain our level of maturity. False humility on the stage of life acts out its spirituality for the world's accolades.

"These rules, which have to do with things that are all destined to perish with use, are based on merely human commands and teachings. Such regulations indeed have an appearance of wisdom, with their self-imposed worship, their false humility and their harsh treatment of the body, but they lack any value in restraining sensual indulgence" (Colossians 2:22-23). True humility seeks only to deflect glory back to God's glory.

However—when all is said and done—living for an audience of one insists on intense intimacy with Jesus Christ, so that we naturally follow His lead. It is like an eloquent dance rendition, where He leads and we follow. Some steps are new and awkward, while other moves are comfortable and unconscious. If we dance with Jesus before others, He will amuse them most, as He leads us into His will. True humility follows Christ's lead.

Lastly, learning to live for an audience of one means to give away recognition and resist taking credit. For example, at work give the team credit for success and take responsibility for failure. At home quietly serve behind the scenes without a worry about who gets the recognition for the house chores. Most of all minister for Christ's kingdom, so your kingdom fades away and His becomes full center. An audience of one pleases the One.

Joseph revealed his devotion to an audience of one with the Lord when he declared, "How then could I do such a wicked thing and sin against God" (Genesis 39:9b)?"

Do I live unashamedly for an audience of one? What competing audience can I dismiss?

Related Readings: 2 Chronicles 32:12; Isaiah 65:16; John 17:1-5; Colossians 2:18

17

Grow Old Together

Even to your old age and gray hairs I am He, I am He who will
sustain you. I have made you and I will carry you;
I will sustain you and I will rescue you.
Isaiah 46:4

There is a relational richness that comes from growing old together. It may be parents, a spouse, children, siblings, friends, church acquaintances or a work associate that contributes to a caring community. Regardless of the source of relational fulfillment it brings to life the Lord's creative design of intentionality in doing life together.

We are not created by our heavenly Father to be isolated and insecure. His plan is for us is to engage with each other in meaningful conversations, patient prayer, loving service and relaxing recreation. Families and friends who grow old together are able to work through conflict, overcome obstacles, serve unselfishly and celebrate God's faithfulness.

"I will sing of the LORD's great love forever; with my mouth I will make your faithfulness known through all generations" (Psalm 89:1b).

Perhaps you and your spouse pray for three other couples with whom you can invest intentional time in fun, fellowship and going deeper with the Lord. They are in a similar season of life as you, so you are able to walk together with empathetic understanding and genuine prayer support. Consider a monthly dinner with games, a Bible study and annual trips together. It.s important to grow old with those whose company you enjoy.

Above all else, grow old with God. The Lord longs to be there for you in the ups and downs of life. His strength sustains you, His compassion carries you and His righteousness rescues you. Every day with Jesus grows sweeter than the day before for the Christian who grows old with grace. God does not give up on you and neither should you.

"The LORD rewards everyone for their righteousness and faithfulness" (1 Samuel 26:23a).

Enjoy the Lord's ever growing influence in your life. Each season of service for your Savior is meant to draw you into more intense intimacy and love. Understanding and accepting Christ's unconditional acceptance and love gives you peace and security to relax in His righteous arms. His aging process gives you permission to be yourself. Relational richness comes from growing old with Christ and with His trusted friends.

"Therefore, my brothers and sisters, you whom I love and long for, my joy and crown, stand firm in the Lord in this way, dear friends" (Philippians 4:1)!

Am I intentional in growing old well with the Lord, friends and family?

Related Readings: Psalm 92:14; Ecclesiastes 4:12; Acts 2:46; 3 John 1:14

18

Meaningful Marriage

"Haven't you read," he replied, "that at the beginning the Creator 'made them male and female,' and said, 'For this reason a man will leave his father and mother and be united to his wife, and the two will become one flesh'? So they are no longer two, but one flesh. Therefore what God has joined together, let no one separate."
Matthew 19:4-6

Marriage means something, because God says it means something. He invented marriage and as the inventor is very proud of His creation. The Lord's primary purpose of a man and a woman coming together in Holy matrimony is to glorify Him. Thus a marriage built on Christ points people to His character and to His perspective on relationships.

For example God's definition of love is active and other centered, so when we read "love is kind" (1 Corinthians 13:4), we express a kind and caring attitude toward our spouse. There is a culture of humility in meaningful marriages that is quick to put the other person's needs before our own. A fulfilling marriage first follows Christ's commands.

"It does not dishonor others, it is not self-seeking, it is not easily angered, it keeps no record of wrongs" (1 Corinthians 13:5). Love looks for ways to love like God loves.

Moreover, a meaningful marriage is made up of a man and woman who are intentional in their investment in each other. A husband cherishes his wife when he prays for her to grow in God's grace and when he seeks her counsel and advice. A wife honors her husband when she prays for him to grow in God's wisdom and when she sees him as the spiritual leader. A marriage of significance is one that plans and prepares on purpose.

"But the plans of the LORD stand firm forever, the purposes of His heart through all generations" (Psalm 33:11).

Wise are the woman and man who learn and discern the Lord's purpose for marriage and then plan to live it out. So with bold humility hitch your marriage to heaven's tractor of trust. The ride is not always smooth and easy, but it is a great adventure with Jesus and your best friend. Ride out the rough spots by faith and forgiveness—and celebrate God's goodness along the way. A meaningful marriage is fun and fulfilling for Christ's sake.

"It always protects, always trusts, always hopes, always perseveres. Love never fails" (1 Corinthians 13:7-8).

How can I make my marriage more meaningful? Have I surrendered to Christ's Lordship?

Related Readings: Joshua 15:16-17; Nehemiah 13:26; Ephesians 5:33; Philippians 2:13

19

Reviving The Soul

The law of the LORD is perfect, reviving the soul.
The statutes of the LORD are trustworthy, making wise the simple.
Psalm 19:7

From time to time our soul needs a revival that only the Word of God can create. Our soul becomes soiled from working in the garden of everyday life, but the washing of the Word removes the impediments to our intimacy with Christ. "How can a young man keep his way pure? By living according to your word" (Psalm 119:9). His commands cleanse.

Our soul can go into a slump like an athlete who is no longer able to execute. So consider a change in your religious routine. Begin journaling or praying out loud the Psalms. Indeed it is during this funk in our faith that the fire from God's word can remove our apathetic attitudes. "Is not My word like fire," declares the LORD, "and like a hammer that breaks a rock in pieces" (Jeremiah 23:29). His word burns away bad attitudes.

How is the state of your soul? Do you have energy for eternal matters? Are you motivated to meditate on the Bible? The incorruptible Word of God works wonders on a weary soul. It purifies and solicits salvation. "Since you have purified your souls in obeying the truth through the Spirit in sincere love of the brethren, love one another fervently with a pure heart, having been born again, not of corruptible seed but incorruptible, through the word of God which lives and abides forever" (1 Peter 1:22-23, NKJV).

Once your soul is revived, your mind is ready to receive wisdom. Your revitalized relationship with Jesus is a launching pad to process His precepts. The Holy Spirit breathes life into your faith so you can embrace and understand Holy Scripture. The renewed spirit is like a smorgasbord for a famished friend whom you invite over for a holiday feast. Let Scripture stimulate your soul and you will grow stronger.

"But his delight is in the law of the LORD, and on his law he meditates day and night. He is like a tree planted by streams of water, which yields its fruit in season and whose leaf does not wither. Whatever he does prospers" (Psalm 1:2-3).

Am I committed to my soul's care? What does my soul need to grow strong and sure?

Related Readings: 2 Kings 23:25; Psalm 42:5-7; Matthew 16:26; Hebrews 4:12

Secret to Happiness

Praise the LORD. Blessed are those who fear the LORD,
who find great delight in his commands.
Psalm 112:1

Praise to the Lord and fear of the Lord are foundational for a fulfilling life. This is the focus of a child of God in love with and loyal to his or her heavenly Father. Worship of Jesus causes the eyes of faith to see Him in His Shekinah glory. His great love secures the soul and His hallowed holiness pierces the heart—resulting in joy and reverence for God.

Moses encountered God at the burning bush, "Do not come any closer," God said. "Take off your sandals, for the place where you are standing is holy ground." Then he said, "I am the God of your father, the God of Abraham, the God of Isaac and the God of Jacob." At this, Moses hid his face, because he was afraid to look at God" (Exodus 3:5-6).

When Christ is the core of a belief system then the natural outcome is peace, joy and happiness. Jesus gives His children His promises so we can walk by faith, trusting that He will do what He said He would do. For example, lasting peace and calm only comes from Christ. Jesus gives us peace of mind, when others angrily give us a piece of their mind. Happiness comes from resting in eternal expectations, not craving earthly ones.

Jesus said, "Very truly I tell you, you will weep and mourn while the world rejoices. You will grieve, but your grief will turn to joy... Now is your time of grief, but I will see you again and you will rejoice, and no one will take away your joy" (John 16:20, 22).

It's in the presence of Jesus that joy wells up in our inner being. Circumstances or any other menacing culprits cannot take His happiness away. We bow our head in fear of the Lord and then lift our eyes toward heaven in worship of the Lord. In worship, as we are overwhelmed by His majestic glory, we are delighted to follow Christ's commands.

Blessed, happy, fortunate, prosperous, and enviable is the one—"Whose delight is in the law of the LORD, and who meditates on his law day and night" (Psalm 1:2)

What is the secret to happiness in this life? It is holding with an open hand the temporal and grasping with a firm hand of faith the eternal. It is an unwavering focus on God and not being disillusioned by other well meaning and not so well meaning Christians. If your joy is gone, replace your fears with the fear of the Lord. Joy follows submission to Jesus.

"As Jesus was saying these things, a woman in the crowd called out, "Blessed is the mother who gave you birth and nursed you." He replied, "Blessed rather are those who hear the word of God and obey it" (Luke 11:27-28).

Am I happy over what brings happiness to the Lord's heart? Do I joyfully obey Jesus?

Related Readings: 1 Samuel 12:14; Psalm 119:166; John 16:33; 3 John 1:1-4

Pray About That

Pray that the LORD your God will tell us where we should go
and what we should do.
Jeremiah 42:3

There is wisdom in praying about "that", whatever "that" may mean. It may mean waiting on marriage because one parent has yet to bless the engagement. "That" could represent a check in your spirit over a business deal or an additional financial obligation. Praying about "that" is the Lord's way to protect, preserve and provide for His children.

What are you currently facing that needs your prayerful attention? Perhaps it's a career transition—pray about that, considering changing churches—pray about that, tempted to quit school—pray about that, or weighing an opportunity to volunteer—pray about that. Prayerfully ask, "What does the Lord want for my life and what's best for His kingdom?"

"Then you will call on me and come and pray to me, and I will listen to you. You will seek me and find me when you seek me with all your heart" (Jeremiah 29:12-13).

It's in the discipline of waiting that we discern the best course of action. Consider cloistering yourself with Christ for twenty-four hours, just to listen and learn. It is rare that prayer is a waste of time—indeed it saves time. When you pray about "that," you allow the Holy Spirit to tap on the brakes of your busy life. Slow down and listen to Him.

Prayer positions you to be productive in the ways of God. Abraham's senior servant experienced this, "Then he prayed, "LORD, God of my master Abraham, make me successful today, and show kindness to my master Abraham" (Genesis 24:12).

When you, your family, your church, your company or your ministry prays about "that," you receive liability insurance for your life from the Lord. Where He leads, He commits to provide. Where He reroutes, He creates the necessary resources. Where He shuts doors, He opens another with greater Kingdom possibilities. So, pray about that knot in your stomach and watch Him free you in effective service for your Savior Jesus.

"Lord, let Your ear be attentive to the prayer of this Your servant and to the prayer of Your servants who delight in revering your name. Give Your servant success today by granting him favor in the presence of this man" (Nehemiah 1:11).

What am I facing that needs my patient prayers? Who can I engage to pray with me?

Related Readings: Ezra 8:23; Daniel 9:20; Luke 22:40-46; Acts 4:23-31

22

A Mother's Prayer

I prayed for this child, and the LORD has granted me what I asked of him. So now I
give him to the LORD. For his whole life he will be given over to the LORD.
And he worshiped the LORD there.
1 Samuel 1:27-28

A mother who prays causes Satan to shudder and his demons to take notice. It is her
steady stream of supplications to her Savior Jesus that garners the attention of God.
Dad may not be around, but her Heavenly Father is there for wisdom and encouragement. She knows the Lord understands, so she seeks Him for grace and comfort. The
prayer of a mom punctures the portals of heaven with passionate petitions that
provide her peace.

She may aspire to be a mother, but is struggling with the ability to conceive. Her heart
breaks for the opportunity to be with child. Her prayers are pregnant with the desire to
become pregnant, and Christ the giver of life listens compassionately and patiently to
her pleas. A barren womb is meant to walk with the Lord during this time of feeling failure and rejection. So she prays for a child, and in the process He loves on His child.

A mother's prayers mark her family with faith and trust in God. Her overflow of mercy
and grace is a reminder that Jesus is the 'author and finisher' of the family's faith. The
fruit from her prayers personify Christ's character, and hell clamors at the calm
requests from a mom who trusts God. They pray for their children to obey and worship
the Lord, and for their husband to fear God, hate sin and love people. A mom's prayer
matters.

Lastly, consider a prayer journal to capture Christ's faithfulness to your faith appeals.
Pray for your children by name and lift each of their unique needs to the Lord. Pray for
your husband's submission to the accountability of Almighty God. Indeed, a wise
mother's first concern is prayer in Jesus name.

"Do not be anxious about anything, but in everything, by prayer and petition, with thanksgiving, present your requests to God" (Philippians 4:6).

Do I constantly worry, or do I apply that same energy in passionate prayer?'

Related Readings: Psalm 66:16-19; Isaiah 28:9; Luke 22:2-3; Acts 1:14

23

Noble Wife

A wife of noble character is her husband's crown,
but a disgraceful wife is a decay to his bones.
Proverbs 12:4

Why are certain wives attractive, and others unattractive? Why do you enjoy the company of some, but avoid the company of others? A wife of noble character is attractive, because she aspires to obey Almighty God. She is a joy to be around, as she enjoys being in the presence of the Lord. Her first allegiance is to her Savior Jesus Christ, exhibited by her regal appearance and respectful responses. God has first place in her heart.

Her husband takes pride in his wife, because she can be trusted in all household matters and financial management. She follows her husband's leadership by faith. She entrusts him under the authority of God to hold him accountable. A wife of noble character knows how to prayerfully ask challenging questions of her man, without usurping his leadership. She is strong and gracious, bold and beautiful, firm and friendly, and faithful and loving.

Her children are loved when they are unlovely, and disciplined when they behave badly. They know their mom cares, even when she gets carried away in her correction. A wife of noble character is a model of motherhood for her daughters, and an example of whom her sons should marry. She is wise to honor her husband in front of the children, especially when they disagree. Her character is a compass for the actions of her kids.

Lastly, a wife of noble character is not afraid to mentor and encourage other wives. Not with a superior spirit, but with an attitude of meekness and brokenness. She quickly admits to her past mistakes, so to save some young women from repeating the hurt and heartache. A student she remains, even while she endeavors to teach and train. Wisdom is worn around her words with humility and grace.

The Bible says, "She is worth far more than rubies" (Proverbs 31:10b).

"Lord, how would you have me grow as a wife and a mother of character?"

Related Readings: Genesis 2:18-24; Ruth 3:11; 1 Corinthians 11:7-11; 1 Timothy 5:2

24

Empty Nest

Where there are no oxen, the manger is empty,
but from the strength of an ox comes an abundant harvest.
Proverbs 14:4

How do you feel since your home has become empty of children? Mad, sad, glad, lonely, without purpose or freed up may all be legitimate emotions you are processing. You have raised them well and now they are off on their own. You are proud of them, but you miss them. They call from college (especially daughters), but it's not the same. It is not easy to export your 'babies' into adulthood, however this is their faith walk to really know God.

We raise them the best we know how: with love, discipline and belief in Jesus Christ. Sometimes they frustrate us by not cleaning their 'crib' (room), like an animal in a barn they can be messy and smelly. There are days you want a little peace and quiet, because they are angry and loud when fighting with their siblings. But the empty nest is void of noise; the kids are nowhere to be found, so enjoy them while you can.

You send them off to grow up and gain a heart of gratitude, and by God's grace they will visit with a new sense of appreciation and maturity. Distance causes friendship with your adult child to grow and not be taken for granted. It is harder to keep up and communicate, but in some ways it is more gratifying. You prepared them to leave, so they can cleave to the one the Lord has for them in marriage. Our empty nest is a test of trust in God's plan.

Lastly, engage with your spouse in your empty nest. Do you feel like you have drifted apart over the years? If so, be intentional to gain back the intense intimacy with your best friend. Make these days of marriage your best, because you believe the Lord has given you your lover to grow old together. Anticipate the gift of grandkids, as they will keep you busy and alive. The empty nest is a season to enjoy the fruit of your family.

"A good man leaves an inheritance for his children's children..."(Proverbs 13:22).

How can I prepare my marriage for when my children leave home?

Related Readings: Genesis 7:1; Proverbs 31:15; Matthew 19:5; Acts 10:2

A Mother's Work

She watches over the affairs of her household and does not eat the bread of idleness.
Her children arise and call her blessed; her husband also, and he praises her.
Proverbs 31:27-28

A mother's work is never done. There is always another meal to prepare, a face to wipe, clothes to wash, an errand to run, a room to clean and a dollar to manage. She serves unselfishly like Jesus, "After that, he poured water into a basin and began to wash his disciples' feet, drying them with the towel that was wrapped around him" (John 13:5). A mother's work makes those around her look good. She is God's chosen one in the home.

The law of love and kindness is written on her heart, but some days it's hard to have the right attitude. The work can become laborious, monotonous and taken for granted. It is at this point of feeling unappreciated that a wise mom reminds herself of heaven's applause. She is really serving for an audience of one, her loving Lord. Her Savior Jesus smiles at her service and that's enough. The reward of doing right encourages her heart to do right.

In addition there are the rewards of a child's smile and warm embrace, "Thank you mommy for being my mommy." Or a loving husband who genuinely thanks her and serves his wife by listening, serving and giving praise. She takes pride in her work, because she recognizes everything she has is a gift from God. Her home and family are a reflection of her and her Heavenly Father. She manages the home for her Master's glory.

Lastly, your work is a model for your children to follow. Your actions become a teacher that prepares them for adulthood. Chores done well, create children who work well. Assign them responsibilities so they learn thoroughness, cleanliness and organization. Indeed your work creates calm in the home, like the Lord quiets your soul.

"But I have stilled and quieted my soul; like a weaned child with its mother, like a weaned child is my soul within me" (Psalm 131:2).

Am I content serving my family for Christ's sake?"

Related Readings: Proverbs 4:3; Proverbs 31:10-31; 1 Timothy 5:14; Titus 2:4

26

A Working Mother

She considers a field and buys it; out of her earnings she plants a vineyard.
She sets about her work vigorously; her arms are strong for her tasks.
Proverbs 31:16-17

Many moms out of necessity, their choice or a combination of both, work outside the home. God has gifted them to invest in the marketplace in a manner that is productive in business and that blesses their home. It is not easy to juggle two full time jobs, but Christ gives them the grace to carry on. Single moms in particular face challenges most of us cannot understand. They need prayer, encouragement, strength and support.

Who do you know who is a single mom? How can you serve them? Maybe an anonymous financial gift, or involve your children in helping with her yard work. A woman who carries all the domestic and marketplace responsibilities needs a community of Christ followers, as friends and confidants. If you are a child of a single mom take the initiative to work around the house and outside the home. Support her with service.

Moreover, do you see your workplace as your ministry, or just a way to make a living? Working moms have a unique opportunity to represent Christ in their career. People will ask, "How do you balance work and home responsibilities?" This is an open door to brag on your husband's support, and describe the importance of faith in the Lord. "If someone asks about your Christian hope, always be ready to explain it" (1 Peter 3:15 NLT).

Working mothers bring grace, wisdom and stability to work environments. If you are an employer encourage them with flexible time schedules and bonuses for a job well done. Facilitate for them a career culture that keeps family first when life-work priorities clash. Working moms deserve recognition and reward. Their Savior is smiling and so should we.

"Finally, be strong in the Lord and in the strength of His might" (Ephesians 6:10 NASB).

Whom do I know that I can encourage in her career by connecting her to a mentor?

Related Readings: Psalm 144:12; Jeremiah 32:9; Acts 16:11-40

27

A Mom's Mothering

Near the cross of Jesus stood his mother, his mother's sister, Mary the wife of
Clopas, and Mary Magdalene. When Jesus saw his mother there, and the disciple
whom he loved standing nearby, he said to his mother, "Dear woman, here is
your son," and to the disciple, "Here is your mother."
From that time on, this disciple took her into his home.
John 19:25-27

Moms are magnificent, especially the ones placed in my life by the Lord. My mom, and
the mother of our children in particular, are emissaries of encouragement. They're
messengers of comfort and care. No one loves more unconditionally than mothers.
They see only the good and forget the bad. A mother's love extends way beyond what
is required, into a reservoir of hope.

Furthermore, they are not afraid to speak the truth, laced with an attractive attitude. It
is not unusual for a mom to become their child's best friend. This is a natural outcome
to their acceptance and relational relentlessness. Because their emotional IQ is high,
they are able to discern and remedy heart felt needs in almost an instant. Indeed, they
are compulsive givers with a propensity to out serve everyone.

Lord this outlandish outpouring of love concerns me. It doesn't bother me that they
love so generously. What troubles me is their need for unconditional love. Are moms
being mothered to the extent that their needs are being met? An un-mothered mom is
a good candidate for a miserable mom. If they are not receiving what they need in
emotional and spiritual support, they wither under the pressure. Like a flower in an
arid climate, they need the moist love, nurture and security of the their Savior Jesus.

Lastly, they value being valued, and desire acceptance. They are secure living in
security, and long to be loved. Lord, lead me to model this for my mom and the mother
of our children. Show me how to shower on them, what they have rained upon relationships season after season in unselfish service. 'I want to give back to them in the same
way they have given to me and our children'. 'I long for the Lord to bless moms!'

"Her children arise and call her blessed; her husband also, and he praises her..." (Proverbs 31:28).

How can I love on my mom or another mom who needs encouraging?

Related Readings: Ruth 1:22; 1 Timothy 5:4; 2 Timothy 1:5; Titus 2:2-4

28

A New Baby

A woman giving birth to a child has pain because her time has come;
but when her baby is born she forgets the anguish
because of her joy that a child is born into the world.
John 16:21

A new baby is a natural experience with a supernatural explanation. It is God's reminder of His incredible grace and gift of life. You can't keep from staring at their little chubby fingers and their pinkish spotted back and belly. They have the scent of freshness straight from their Heavenly Father's handiwork. A new baby brings joy and attention to Jesus.

A new baby's eyes have the look of the Lord's love. Their coos are the sounds of their Savior's caring communication. Their cries resound with a need for Christ. Their tender feet are a foreshadowing of walking with Jesus through the up's and down's of life. A new baby brings back memories of a mom in pain who is quickly overcome by joy. Mostly a new baby illustrates God's new birth of a soul. It's delivered into eternal life.

A new baby points to the new birth. Just as the Lord delivers a physical life, so a spiritual birth is God's supernatural act of a soul's salvation. Jesus described it the best, "Unless a person submits to this original creation—the 'wind-hovering-over-the-water' creation, the invisible moving the visible, a baptism into a new life—it's not possible to enter God's kingdom. When you look at a baby, it's just that: a body you can look at and touch. But the person who takes shape within is formed by something you can't see and touch—the Spirit—and becomes a living spirit" (John 3:5-6, TM).

Lastly, a new baby brings magnificent joy. The mom and dad are full of joy. The grand parents are teary eyed with joy, and the aunts and uncles are smitten by simple joy. Smiles cannot be contained around the mesmerizing affect of an infant. Prayers launch moment by moment from grateful hearts to heaven.

Thank God for a new baby, and thank Him even more for those born into His Kingdom. Jesus said, "I tell you that in the same way there will be more rejoicing in heaven over one sinner who repents than over ninety-nine righteous persons who do not need to repent" (Luke 15:7).

Does my excitement for those born into God's family bring pure joy and praise to the Lord?

Related Readings: Genesis 3:16; Psalm 113:9; Luke 1:57-58; Galatians 4:27

29

Grateful Children

I have no greater joy than to hear that my children are walking in the truth.
3 John 1:4

Gratitude is a wonderful gift we can give to our children and our children can give to us. It brings overwhelming joy to the heart of a parent when they witness an appreciative child. When they hear "thank you," "you are welcome" and "how can I help", it is music to the ears of mom and dad who long for their loved ones to grow into grateful adults.

Thankfulness is a vaccine against selfishness and discontentment. Children and teenagers who understand and apply appreciation are quick to serve others and not demand their needs or wants be met. They take to heart what God expects of His sons and daughters, "Do nothing out of selfish ambition or vain conceit, but in humility consider others better than yourselves. Each of you should look not only to your own interests, but also to the interests of others" (Philippians 2:3-4). Gratitude leads to a Christ-like attitude.

So, how can you help your child learn to live a life of thanksgiving and gratitude? What does it take for a teenager to meet the needs of others before addressing their own needs? One thought is to begin early teaching your child the value of hard work. Assign them chores and then pay them when the job is completed with excellence. Then train them to divide their money into the categories of save, give and spend. When they invest time and energy into a meaningful outcome they are much more appreciative of the money.

Perhaps you accompany them to feed the homeless, care for a family in financial distress or visit those confined to jail. You may decide on a family mission trip over-seas. It may be a construction project, evangelism outreach or loving on orphans.

Contentment and gratitude will erupt from the heart of your child, when they engage people who smile in the face of ugly circumstances. They see first hand that joy comes from Jesus not stuff.

Therefore be intentional about modeling appreciation in front of your offspring. Be quick to thank God and others, while slow to complain. Grateful children are attractive and pleasant to be around. Their appreciative attitude will serve them well the rest of life.

"Your attitude should be the same as that of Christ Jesus: Who, being in very nature God, did not consider equality with God something to be grasped, but made himself nothing, taking the very nature of a servant, being made in human likeness. And being found in appearance as a man, he humbled himself and became obedient to death— even death on a cross!" (Philippians 2:5-8)

How can I model an attitude of gratitude in front of my children? What can we do as a family to learn appreciation and experience contentment?

Related Readings: Deuteronomy 4:9-10; Psalm 34:11; Proverbs 22:6; Ephesians 6:4

30

Humor Helps

A cheerful disposition is good for your health; gloom and doom leave you bone-tired.
Proverbs 17:22 (The Message)

Humor is shock absorbers for your soul. 'A person without a sense of humor is like a wagon without springs, jolted by every pebble on the road.' Humor is heaven's helpmate to get you through difficulties. It's healthful to be cheerful. Therefore, chose a belly laugh over high blood pressure, a smile over a stroke and a grin over grouchiness. How is your humor quotient? Do you laugh a lot or a little? Make humor a habit of your holiness.

Go ahead and smile, you'll feel better. Laughter longs to be let loose, like a closely confined kite waffling in the wind ready to take off. It's exhilarating to experience its liberation. Humor releases relationships to remember why they liked each other in the first place, and to reflect on their gratitude to God. "Our mouths were filled with laughter, our tongues with songs of joy. Then it was said among the nations, "The LORD has done great things for them" (Psalm 126:2).

However, a frown is fatiguing. It is wearisome to worry under the weight of responsibilities that are not yours. Humor is not irresponsible, but it does prepare you to winnow out what's important from what's urgent. Another's cares are not your crisis, so help them laugh out loud. They might take themselves less seriously and God more. A smile says I care. I think the best of you. "A cheerful heart brings a smile to your face; a sad heart makes it hard to get through the day" (Proverbs 15:13, TM).

Lastly don't joke about Jesus, but be jovial as His ambassador. Joy attracts new and old Jesus followers. They see Christ in your cheery countenance. Humor is heaven's tool for evangelism and discipleship. It is a safe and beautiful bridge from unbelief to belief. Do I attract people with my fun-loving faith, or are they repelled by my grumbling and negative attitudes? Humor harnesses your Master's might.

"Do not be grieved, for the joy of the LORD is your strength" (Nehemiah 8:10b NASB).

How can I not take myself too seriously and the Lord more seriously?

Related Readings: Job 8:21; Ecclesiastes 9:7-9; Luke 15:24; John 16:33

WHAT READERS ARE SAYING
ABOUT WISDOM HUNTERS

Thank you for sharing this with us today. It could not of come at a better time. I have had a very rough day and this is the first time anyone ever explained it so plainly. So thank you and God bless. – NJ

I look forward to reading Wisdom Hunters every morning to reinforce and strengthen my faith. Thank you for providing such a wonderful beginning to your reader's days. – Kathy

THANK YOU for sharing this personal story as a post. It helps me tremendously to know & see how others 'wrestle with God' and themselves in trying to let go of wounds inflicted by those who were supposed to protect us and love us the most. It also shows how 'letting go & letting GOD' can bring SALVATION to those we SO love, but don't know how to reach. Giving it up to God can change our perception of rejection, (something I struggle MIGHTILY with), to relationship! BLESS YOU! – Teresa

You have no idea how I look forward to getting your devotionals every morning. They are wise, and I find that they ground me for the day (and that takes a few good anchors!). Thank you very much. – Jane

I did not sleep well last night due to a situation with my son and soon to be daughter-in-law. I woke up several times with things on my mind. I asked the Lord, what is it? Was it me? Am I this bad of a Christian? Wisdom Hunters is God's voice today of Him answering and I need to heed it! Thank you Mr. Boyd for being a vessel used by the Almighty! God Bless you and yours. – Jenny

I so enjoy your devotionals. As soon as we moved anticipating the next journey of retirement I was diagnosed with M.S. so the journey for both of us has become a far different one then we had anticipated. These devotionals really help me to keep to the Lord. It is hard and many times the devil is right on my doorstep but I keep perservering. Your part it in with these devotionals gives me a chance to breathe God's word into me – So thanks. – Diane

Love these insights and Scriptural readings. This one on giving up all – only to have some returned in blessings – and experiencing what we hang on tightly to taken from us is sobering and challenging. Thanks. – Carroll

An extremely valuable person in my life, forwarded todays, Heartfelt Forgiveness. I was speechless, to not only have her forgive me, but also the chance to read such a strong message. This person who sent this to me, really brought me back to my faith because I had pulled away after my divorce. To wake up and be "forgiven" brought me to tears, such an amazing way to start my day and get this message from someone that I thought was gone from my life since last August. I have prayed daily this person would not only forgive me but also allow me to show her just how much I respect, trust and love. – Alan

Every day that I read Wisdom Hunters I am   blessed. God is using you in a mighty way to challenge us daily to think of our Lord and Savior Jesus Christ and to think of others before ourselves. My husband and I have used them as quotes or messages during our speaking engagents for them to encourage others as well. Thank you!!!! – Rachel

Just want to say thank you for sharing the obvious gift God has given you. Your writing and deep insight challenge me to go higher and deeper in my walk with Christ. I began receiving your daily devotions a few weeks ago and already I feel the pruning taking place in my life. – Sonya

Mr. Bailey, Thank you for the word of encouragement this morning. The Lord brought me into these words of wisdom just in time. Praise be to our Lord Jesus Christ. God bless you and keep you. - Marguerite

BECOMING A DISCIPLE
OF JESUS CHRIST

My journey that led me to God covered a span of 19 years, before I truly understood my need for His love and forgiveness in a personal relationship with Jesus Christ. Along this path of spiritual awakening, God placed many people along the way as spiritual guideposts directing me toward Him.

Initially it was my mother who took me to church at age 12 so I could learn about faith through the confirmation process. My grandmother was a role model in her walk with Jesus by being kind and generous to all she encountered. Once in college, I began attending church with Rita (my future wife) and her family.

It was then that relevant weekly teaching from an ancient book—the Bible—began to answer many of life's questions. It intrigued me: What is God's plan for my life? Who is Jesus Christ? What are sin, salvation, heaven and hell? How can I live an - abundant life of forgiveness, joy and love?

So, the Lord found me first with His incredible love and when I surrendered in repentance and faith in Jesus, I found Him. For two years a businessman in our church showed me how to grow in grace through Bible study, prayer, faith sharing and service to others. I still discover each day more of God's great love and His new mercies.

Below is an outline for finding God and becoming a disciple of Jesus:

1. BELIEVE: "If you declare with your mouth, "Jesus is Lord," and believe in your heart that God raised him from the dead, you will be saved" (Romans 10:9). Belief in Jesus Christ as your Savior and Lord gives you eternal life in heaven.

2. REPENT AND BE BAPTIZED: "Peter replied, 'Repent and be baptized, every one of you, in the name of Jesus Christ for the forgiveness of your sins. And you will receive the gift of the Holy Spirit'" (Acts 2:38). Repentance means you turn from your sin and publically confess Christ in baptism.

3. OBEY: "Jesus replied, 'Anyone who loves me will obey my teaching. My Father will love them, and we will come to them and make our home with them'" (John 14:23). Obedience is an indicator of our love for the Lord Jesus and His presence in our life.

4. WORSHIP, PRAYER, COMMUNITY, EVANGELISM AND STUDY: "Every day they continued to meet together in the temple courts. They broke bread in their homes and ate together with glad and sincere hearts, praising God and enjoying the favor of all the people. And the Lord added to their number daily those who were being saved" (Acts 2:46-47). Worship and prayer are our expressions of gratitude and honor to God and our dependence on His grace. Community and evangelism are our accountability to Christians and compassion for non-Christians. Study to apply the knowledge, understanding, and wisdom of God.

5. LOVE GOD: "Jesus replied: 'Love the Lord your God with all your heart and with all your soul and with all your mind.' This is the first and greatest commandment" (Matthew 22:37-38). Intimacy with the almighty God is a growing and loving relationship. We are loved by Him, so we can love others and be empowered by the Holy Spirit to obey His commands.

6. LOVE PEOPLE: "And the second is like it: 'Love your neighbor as yourself'" (Matthew 22:39). Loving people is an outflow of the love for our heavenly Father. We are able to love because He first loved us.

7. MAKE DISCIPLES: "And the things you have heard me say in the presence of many witnesses entrust to reliable people who will also be qualified to teach others" (2 Timothy 2:2). The reason we disciple others is because we are extremely grateful to God and to those who disciple us, and we want to obey Christ's last instructions before going to heaven.

Daily Wisdom in Your Inbox... A Free Subscription: www.wisdomhunters.com

MEET THE AUTHOR

Boyd Bailey

Boyd Bailey, the author of Wisdom Hunters devotionals, is the founder of Wisdom Hunters, Inc., an Atlanta-based ministry created to encourage Christians (a.k.a wisdom hunters) to *apply God's unchanging Truth in a changing world.*

By God's grace, Boyd has impacted wisdom hunters in over 86 countries across the globe through the Wisdom Hunters daily devotion, wisdomhunters.com devotional blog and devotional books.

For over 30 years Boyd Bailey has passionately pursued wisdom through his career in fulltime ministry, executive coaching, and mentoring.

Since becoming a Christian at the age of 19, Boyd begins each day as a wisdom hunter, diligently searching for Truth in scripture, and through God's grace, applying it to his life.

These raw, 'real time' reflections from his personal time with the Lord, are now impacting over 111,000 people through the Wisdom Hunters Daily Devotion email. In addition to the daily devotion, Boyd has authored nine devotional books: *Infusion*, a 90-day devotional, *Seeking Daily the Heart of God Vol I & II*, 365-day devotionals *Seeking God in the Proverbs*, a 90-day devotional and *Seeking God in the Psalms*, a 90-day devotional along with several 30-day devotional e-Books on topics such as *Wisdom for Fathers*, *Wisdom for Mothers*, *Wisdom for Graduates*, and *Wisdom for Marriage.*

In addition to Wisdom Hunters, Boyd is the co-founder and CEO of Ministry Ventures, a faith based non-profit, where he has trained and coached over 1000 ministries in the best practices of prayer, board, ministry models, administration and fundraising. Prior to Ministry Ventures, Boyd was the National Director for Crown Financial Ministries and an Associate Pastor at First Baptist Church of Atlanta. Boyd serves on numerous boards including Ministry Ventures, Wisdom Hunters, Atlanta Mission, Souly Business and Blue Print for Life.

Boyd received his Bachelor of Arts from Jacksonville State University and his Masters of Divinity from Southwestern Seminary. He and Rita, his wife of 30 plus years, live in Roswell, Georgia and are blessed with four daughters, three sons-in-law who love Jesus, two granddaughters and two grandsons. Boyd and Rita enjoy missions and investing in young couples, as well as hiking, reading, traveling, working through their bucket list, watching college football, and hanging out with their kids and grand kids when ever possible.